15-Minute Life-Shifting Prayer

Who God Is

Joel B. Stratton

WESTBOW
PRESS®
A DIVISION OF THOMAS NELSON
& ZONDERVAN

WestBow Press books may be ordered through booksellers or by contacting:

WestBow Press
A Division of Thomas Nelson & Zondervan
1663 Liberty Drive
Bloomington, IN 47403
www.westbowpress.com
844-714-3454

ISBN: 978-1-6642-0080-7 (sc)
ISBN: 978-1-6642-0081-4 (hc)
ISBN: 978-1-6642-0079-1 (e)

Library of Congress Control Number: 2020914211

Print information available on the last page.

WestBow Press rev. date: 08/21/2020

Contents

Dedication...2

Acknowledgments...3

Preface..4

Introduction...5

Prayer...6

Author's Note 98

Conclusion...99

Do You Have a Personal Relationship with God?............................101

Booking Information..103

Dedication

To Mom and Dad—or as we kids call them, Momma and Papa. They both exude what it means to be Christ followers. I truly could not have asked God for better parents and better examples than these two. Whether believing God for a lifesaving miracle or believing that God would provide supernatural provision so we could have our next meal, they have stayed firm to God's promises and have led us to know the true power of our living God. I love you both more than words can express.

Acknowledgments

God my Father, God the Son, and God the Holy Spirit. I've only just begun to outwardly express my love toward You! I know that there are new and exciting ways to love You each and every day as I continue to find out more about You. I wake up differently now, all because of You. I have a new purpose, a new mission, and a new way of life because of You. You are my all, and I love You! Thanks for being a good Father!

Two people I have never met but who have genuinely changed my life are the following:

✝ Rodney Howard-Brown. Although I do not know him personally, his ministry has radically changed my life! Because of his obedience to the Lord and the example that he and his church members have lived, I know that God loves me unconditionally. I have *pressed **in*** to God now that I'm connected with The River Church of Tampa Bay. So thank you, church!

✝ Andrew Wommack has played a major role in my life as well. His consistency on the topic of prayer has developed and continues to develop my prayer life each and every day. Thank you for being knowledgeable and being used of God to speak into my life. You have shown me how confusing we as a church have made our prayer life. We have been deceived into thinking that God doesn't answer our prayers or picks and chooses which prayers He will answer. That's just not the case. He has answered all of our prayers! To put it bluntly, it's either us or the enemy that gets in our way. It's up to us to speak to our mountains and take what is rightfully ours from God Himself! Amen!

Preface

Many of you may have had times in your life when you can look back on and know that God has brought you through tough situations. I'm sure that when you were in the middle of them, you thought there was no way out. You may be in a situation currently and see zero open doors to go through and only see paths of destruction ahead of you. This is an absolute lie of the enemy! I want to encourage you that even in my current situation as I'm writing this, I've also been lied to and told that there was no way out. I want to encourage you to grab hold of the absolute power of prayer! Unfortunately, even though I've grown up in the church, I'd never unlocked the fullness of how God intended us to pray until recently. I'm telling you, and I promise you, that I'm a different man because of what I've been practicing in my own prayer life. I have a new power that is a heavenly power that all believers can have and have been promised by God Himself (see Matthew 28:18–20). I know that some may read scripture references regarding the enemy is here to steal, kill, and destroy. You may say that you are not afraid of the devil, but the way you live your life says otherwise. I'm telling you the enemy is not on our level! He is beneath us! He cannot touch us if we are truly living in communion/prayer with God throughout every day. Yes, you can be in constant interaction with our living God and gain understanding of **Who God Is** more and more, each and every day (see Mark 16:15–18).

My questions to you are these: How do we approach God when we pray? Do we just pray a list of requests we need for Him to fix or heal? Do we really press *in* to God out of desperation for a move of His mighty hand? I'm pleading with you to pray differently! Pray with expectancy! Pray with expectation! Pray with anticipation! God has already said that He has healed you. God has already taken care of your fear. God has already taking care of the enemy! He has the victory! All you must do is ask, and it will be given to you! Push yourself *in* to God, and watch Him radically push you to move mountains in your life. Yes, move mountains! You **can** move mountains out of your way! God has given you the authority to take down your mountains! I haven't seen every mountain move yet in my life, but I have a new understanding and a new peace that come only from God Himself. I know without a doubt that my mountains are trembling and will fall! More than ever, we need the heavenly, life-shifting power of **Who God Is**. You **can** and **will** take down strongholds in your life!

Introduction

Within the pages to follow is a twelve-minute prayer—a prayer that is not focused on you but is focused on **Who God Is**. Take this book along with you wherever you go. I passionately believe this is a life-shifting prayer that needs to stay by your side and be your weapon against the attacks of the enemy. I know it seems like a lot of pages to read in one sitting, but it should only take about twelve minutes to read. I encourage you to buy at least two prayer guides so that you can keep one for yourself and have a copy to send other people who may be hurting and need confidence that is found only in God Himself.

Here is how I use the following *15-Minute Life-Shifting Prayer*. I know I just mentioned earlier that it's a twelve-minute prayer and it seemed to be a typo. This was on purpose. This prayer of **Who God Is** will only take you about twelve minutes, but then you have the remaining three minutes to go before God about your own needs. Read this prayer out loud if you can, with passion, enthusiasm, emotion, and excitement! After all, these are all facts as to **Who God Is!** The Bible backs everything up as steadfast truths! I pray this prayer every day because I need His strength. I challenge you to do the same. My challenge to you is to pray this prayer for **seven consecutive days** at first. Allow the presence of God to show you how real and powerful He is. As you read this day-to-day, you will find yourself trusting and believing in what you are reading. Your words, your heart, and your spirit will begin to line up with what you are reading. Again, after you are finished reading and claiming these truths, then go into your own time of prayer. Do not just ask God for your needs to be met; tell your list of needs how to proceed! Tell your hurts and pains to leave! Command your body to be healed! Let your finances know that God has already provided for your needs and more! God has given you this power to overcome anything you may be going through!

Let this be a faith builder for your personal walk with the Lord. And as you build on your faith, I guarantee you that you will see a mighty move of God in your life. Now lift your voice to the Lord, start building on your faith, and enjoy the goodness of our God as you pray this powerful prayer of **Who God Is.**

You are the God of Abraham.

† El Shaddai *(God Almighty)*.
† The God who is more than enough—the all-sufficient one.
† Jehovah Jireh, my provider.
† The God of blessing.

You are the God of Isaac.

† The God of joy.
† The God of laughter.
† The God of blessing.
† You are the God of increase in the time of famine and storm.
† The God who makes a way when there is no way.

You are the God of Jacob.

† The God of grace to those who have been unfaithful.
† The God of mercy.
† You change and renew me.
† You bless me.
† You give me a new name!

The Name above every other name.

—Philippians 2:9 (NIV)

You are Jehovah Rapha.

The God who heals.

You will rescue me; protect me, because I acknowledge Your Name. When I call on You, You will answer. You are my deliverer. You honor me! With long life You will satisfy me and show me Your salvation.

—Psalm 91:14–16 (NIV)

You are Alpha and Omega.

†   You are the beginning and the end.

†   You are the first and last.

†   You are which was, which is, and which is to come.

You are the Lily of the Valley.

† A sweet fragrance, pure and humble.
   (The lily also represents the Second Coming of Christ.)
† You are coming back for me!

You are the Bright and Morning Star.

—Revelation 22:16 (KJV)

You are the Fairest of Ten Thousand.
The most dazzling of all.

—Song of Solomon 5:10 (NIV)

You are the Lion of Judah!
Strength and Power.

—Revelation 5:5 (NIV)

You are the start and the author of life.

—Hebrews 12:2 (NKJV)

God, Your ways are perfect.
Lord, Your words are flawless.

—Psalm 18:30 (NIV)

You are the pearl of great price.
A valuable treasure that needs no polishing.

—Matthew 13:45–46 (NKJV)

You are the rock on which I stand.

—Psalm 18:2 (KJV)

You are the shelter in the time of storm.

—Psalm 27:5 (NIV)

You are my Savior, my Protector, my Redeemer, my Liberator, and my Rescuer.

The Lord is my light and my salvation—
whom shall I fear? The Lord is the stronghold
of my life—of whom shall I be afraid?

—Psalm 27:1 (NIV)

Your name is a strong and mighty
tower in which I run to and take
shelter where I am safe.

—Proverbs 18:10 (KJV)

You are my Island Hideaway! You keep danger far from the shore. You throw garlands of hosannas around my neck.

—Psalm 32:7 (MSG)

You brought Your people out of bondage.

† You delivered them with a strong and mighty hand.
(Exodus 20:2 NIV)

† Even in the place of disobedience, their clothes did not grow old upon them.

† Nor did their feet swell. (Deuteronomy 8:4 NIV)

† You brought them forward with silver and gold.

† There was not one sick or feeble among them. (Psalm 105:37 NIV)

† You brought them out with a pillar of cloud by day and a pillar of fire by night. You are my wall of fire!
(Exodus 13:21 NIV)

† You gave them mana from heaven, and You gave them water from the rock. (Exodus 16:4; 17:1–7 NIV)

† You delivered and brought them out with a great victory.

You are the deliverer.

† You are the one who delivers me out of every affliction, disease, sickness, problem, and disorder.
† Every lie of the enemy.
† I lift my voice. I praise You. I exalt, applaud, revere, respect, admire, and promote You.

A thousand shall fall at Your side,
ten thousand at Your right hand.

*The power of God can bring me near to
danger, and yet keep me far from harm.*

—Psalm 91:7 (KJV)

As You were with Moses, so You are with me.

† Nothing shall stand before me all the days of my life.
† Every place in which the sole of my foot shall tread, You have given it unto me.
† You've given me the land. I will go in and possess it. It's mine.
† You have delivered the enemy into my hand.
† I will go in and take the cities, there's not one city too big. (Joshua 1:1–18 NIV)

You've given Your angels charge over me.

—Psalm 91:11 (NKJV)

You go before me and make
my crooked path straight.

—Isaiah 45:2 (NKJV)

Let God arise and my
enemies be scattered.

—Psalm 68:1 (KJV)

You are my peace.

† My joy.
† My righteousness. *You are all about justice.*
† My king.
† My healer.
† My provider.
† You are the author and the finisher of my faith.

You started it, and You will finish it!

You didn't bring me this far
to leave me now!

—Philippians 1:6 (NIV)

You are the God of David.

✠   You will hand my enemies over to me.

✠   You are my new song every morning.

✠   Your righteousness is like the great mountains. (Psalm 36:6 NKJV)

✠   Lord, You preserve me.

✠   You will make my righteous reward shine like the dawn. (Psalm 37:6 NIV)

✠   You will vindicate, justify, and support me.

You are the God of Shadrach, Meshach, and Abednego.

† My faith and trust in You will keep me safe from the fire as I holdfast *(cling to)* Your powerful name, Jesus.
† My clothes will not even smell like smoke from the fire that my enemies try to throw me into.

You are the God of Daniel.

† I rely solely on Your name.
† You are trustworthy, upright, and reliable.
† You will keep me safe from the jaws of lions who are trying to devour me.
† God, You are sovereign *(supreme)* over all earthly kings.

You are the God of Matthew, Mark, Luke, and John.

† You are no respecter of persons.
† Whether a person is a tax collector, a doctor, a fisherman, or a teenager, You have called everyone and know them by name.
† You are with me to meet my every need.
† You are my healer!

You are the Way Maker.

You are the Miracle Worker.

You are a Promise Keeper.

You are the Light in the darkness.

You wipe away all tears.

You mend the broken heart.

Love the Lord, all His faithful people!
The Lord preserves those who are
true to Him, but the proud He pays
back in full. Be strong and take heart,
all you who hope in the Lord.

—Psalm 31:23–24 (NIV)

You are the answer to it all!

You guide me through
the mountains and the valleys.

—Psalm 139:1–18 (NIV)

Your joy restores my soul.

—Psalm 51:12 (NIV)

With You, I'm not alone.

—Joshua 1:9 (NIV)

We wait in hope for the Lord; He is our help and our shield. In Him our hearts rejoice, for we trust in His holy name. May your unfailing love be with us, Lord, even as we put our hope in You.

—Psalm 33:20–22 (NIV)

You are my comfort and
always hold me close.

—Psalm 23

Your Spirit lives within me, so I
will walk in Your peace.

—Psalm 23

You are my justifier.

† You vindicate, defend, and prove me.
† You validate, support, and confirm me.

You are my advocate.

†   You speak on my behalf.
†   You believe and back me.
†   You campaign me!

You are my strengthener.

—Psalm 46:1–3 (NIV)

You are the door opener. If there is no door to open, You will blow a hole in the wall! You will provide!

The devil may try to flatter me,
but the people who know their
God will firmly resist him.

—Daniel 11:32 (NIV)

The devil is a creation,
but God, You are the Creator.

The devil has a beginning and an end,
but God, You are *the*
beginning and *the* end.

God, You win!

Greater is *he* who is in (me) than
he that is in the world.

—1 John 4:4 (KJV)

The devil and I are not in the same category!

† The first two chapters of Ephesians say that God has raised me up together with Christ and He's put me together with Him, seated in heavenly places with all things under my feet.

† Matthew 28:18–20 says that He's given me all His power and authority in heaven and earth, to go into all the world and preach the Gospel.

† The Bible says that one of the signs that will follow believers in Jesus is that they will cast out devils. When I am doing the works of Jesus, I am casting out devils; devils are not casting me out! (Mark 16:15–18)

You are a multiplier.

—Genesis 22:17; Jeremiah 30:19 (KJV)

Jesus, You promise to me, "If you remain in me and my words remain in you, ask whatever you wish, and it will be done for you. This is to my Father's glory, that you bear much fruit, showing yourselves to be my disciples."

—John 15:7–8 (NIV)

You are my Shepherd.

† You feed me.

† You guide me.

† You shield me.

† I will not lack. (Psalm 23:1 NIV)

† You laid Your life down for me! (John 10:11 NIV)

He tends His flock like a shepherd:
He gathers the lambs in His arms and
carries them close to His heart; He
gently leads those that have young.

—Isaiah 40:11 (NIV)

My enemy may be on the attack, but they cannot touch me because goodness and mercy follow me all the days of my life!

—Psalm 23:6 (NKJV)

You will make me the most prosperous.

† Rich, successful, wealthy, and thriving in all the work of Your hand ...
† You, Lord, delight in me. (Deuteronomy 30:8–9 NIV)

You put me through the fire.

†   You refine, polish, and enhance me.

†   You purge, cleanse, and remove sin from me.

†   You purify and sterilize me.

You bless me and love me!

This is the confidence we have in approaching God: that if we ask anything according to His will, He hears us.

—1 John 5:14 (NIV)

You are the God of Solomon.

† You provide me with a wise and a discerning mind.

† You make me prosper and succeed.

† You make me powerful and give me authority over all my enemies.

God, Your Word says, "If any of you lacks wisdom, you should ask God, who gives generously to all without finding fault, and it will be given to you."

—James 1:5 (NIV)

You are the God who heals!

You are the God who has
given me the victory!

You are the God of the impossible!

You are joy unspeakable and full of glory!

—1 Peter 1:8 (KJV)

The same Spirit that raised Jesus
from the dead lives in me!

—Romans 8:11 (NIV)

Holy Spirit:

† You are my teacher. (John 14:26 NIV)
† You are my advocate. (John 15:26 NIV)
† You are my guide and my intercessor. My mediator. (John 16:13 NIV)
† You are my comforter. (John 14:26 NIV)
† You give me power to overcome sin. (Acts 1:8; 4:31 NIV)
† You give me power to reject temptation. (Romans 15:13 NIV)

God, You said that if I come near to
You, You will come near to me.

—James 4:8 (NIV)

This is the day that the Lord has made!

† I will rejoice and be glad in it! (Psalm 118:24 KJV)

† I'm going to worship You!

† I'm going to praise You in the morning!

† I'm going to praise You in the noontime!

† I'm going to praise You in the evening!

† As long as I have breath, I'm going to praise You!

In Your presence there is fullness of joy; at Your right hand are pleasures forevermore.

—Psalm 16:11 (NKJV)

Jesus, You said, "Come to me, all you who are weary and burdened, and I will give you rest. Take My yoke upon you and learn from Me, for I am gentle and humble in heart, and you will find rest for your souls. For My yoke is easy and My burden is light."

—Matthew 11:28–30 (NIV)

In Your presence is healing!

In Your presence is provision!

In Your presence is everything I need!

You are Emmanuel, "God with us."

When You walk through the door,
the very atmosphere changes!

You set me above my companions
by anointing me with the oil of joy.

—Psalm 45:7 (NIV)

You rescue me because of
Your unfailing love.

—Psalm 44:26 (NIV)

You vindicate me and rescue me from those who are deceitful and wicked.

—Psalm 43:1 (NIV)

No one compares with You!

—Psalm 40:5 (NIV)

That's the God I serve!

I am a Christian! I am the anointed one!

God, move! God, I'm tired of the status quo! Lord, I'm hungry for You. God, come and touch me!

Help me be aligned and united
with You! I want renewal in me!
A revival way of life in me!

Author's Note

Now lift your voice and worship Him! Pray over your specific needs! Take reign over them and receive the Lord's divine answers! In the name of Jesus, it is finished! Amen!

Conclusion

By no means am I saying that this prayer is the only prayer you will ever need. My hope and prayer are that this is just the beginning of a more personal communion with God throughout every second of your every day. Use the extra space on each page to write in your own words about **Who God Is**. The Lord longs to be in communion with you. He doesn't want to just have a few minutes of your day through a daily devotional. God gave me a powerful word one day as I was taking a walk. *God did not start moving in my life until I stopped giving Him five minutes of my day.* Let me explain.

I was your typical Christian who, yes, gave God my five minutes in the morning to read a quick devotional. The devotionals may or may not have had an impact on my day, but I did them, and honestly, most days, I felt that I accomplished my time with God for that day. Throughout the day, I also felt good about asking God for help as different needs came up. I made myself believe that I was communicating with God on a daily basis.

I had an enormous wake-up call when I realized that my world was falling apart around me, and I didn't even know how to pray. I didn't have any power or strength to even begin to comprehend how to approach my mountains that seemed to be growing taller and taller as each day passed. I was crippled! The enemy had me believe through all these years that I had a "relationship" with God and that was enough. In the lowest of lowest valleys is where God was finally able to speak to me through key human individuals He sent to me and opened my spiritual eyes to an amazing, supernatural relationship with my Creator. My Supreme King!

How did I shift to a supernatural relationship?

- **Time**

    You do not get to know someone by just spending a few minutes here and there with that person. You can't know who they are when you are constantly looking at the time. If we are not open to truly be in communion with Him throughout every day, His goodness and mercy for us will not even be on our radar. We will not be able to see what He has for us. He has so much to give us if we would just receive.

- **Understand Who God Is**

  Spend time studying who God is! If you do not understand all that God is and has for you, your spirit will not get excited for what God is going to do through you! This was a game changer for me. The life shift for me happened when I daily told myself about **Who God Is**. The enemy hates this! It reminds him that God has already had victory over him and greater is He who is in me than he who is in the world!

- **Give God Glory in Our Praise and Worship**

  The heavens triumph and move within our praise and worship to our God. Healings, miracles, and a supernatural move of God are waiting to happen within the praises of His people. *So what are you waiting for?*

  Use this guide as a faith builder, a stepping-stone if you will, to launch your faith in a better direction. Build, grow, strengthen, and nurture your faith.

Do You Have a Personal Relationship with God?

Has anyone every told you that God loves you and has an amazing plan for your life? The most important question you will ever face today is if you were to die today, where would you spend eternity? Can you say you would most definitely be in heaven? If you have just answered, "No," "I think so," or "I hope so," let me share with you what the Bible says.

Romans 3:23 says, "For all have sinned and fall short of the glory of God," and Romans 6:23 says, "For the wages of sin is death, but the gift of God is eternal life in Christ Jesus our Lord." The Bible also says in Romans 10:13, "For whosoever shall call upon the name of the Lord shall be saved." This scripture is talking about you! You are the "whosoever"! Today is the day your name can be written into the Lamb's Book of Life. You can be accounted for in heaven! All you must do is ask Jesus for forgiveness of your sin, believe that He is risen from the dead, and ask Him to be the Lord of your life. Ask Him to lead and guide you. It's that simple. If I'm talking to you right now, then as you read this short prayer with me, mean it with everything within you and you will see an immediate miracle in your life. You will be a new creation in Him, and you will be saved from a life of sin and turmoil!

Read this prayer with me:

> Dear Lord Jesus, come into my heart. Forgive me of my sin. Wash me and cleanse me. Set me free. Jesus, thank You for dying on the cross for me. I believe that You are risen from the dead and that You're coming back again for me. Give me a hunger for the things of God and a boldness to share with others what You have done for me. I am saved! I am born again! I am forgiven! And I am on my way to heaven because I have Jesus in my heart! Amen!

If you prayed this prayer for the first time or rededicated your life, I would love to hear from you!
Please email me at joel@iamrescued.com.

Order more books online: www.iamrescued.com/store.

Booking Information

Check us out online for event or Sunday service booking information: www.iamrescued.com/booking-information.

The renewal of our minds starts with our daily time we spend with God. It seems so basic, but so many Christians are missing out on the true supernatural blessing that God wants to pour out on all people. If you want spiritual growth, then you have to have a plan. I would be honored to help you achieve that plan for your congregation. Let us know about your availability, and we will work out the details!

About the Author

Joel Stratton was born and raised in Wisconsin. He has always had a passion for the church and how the "world" perceives the church. Throughout his life trials and tribulations, he has seen God move in supernatural ways and is motivated to share all that God has to offer His people.

"God did not start moving in my life until I stopped giving Him 5 minutes of my day." - Joel B Stratton